OMAR

THE SCEPTER OF THE
KINGDOM

outskirts
press

ACKNOWLEDGEMENTS

I would first like to thank every teacher of the Word of God in prior and present generations that I have had the priviledge of learning from.

A personal thank you goes to Dr. Gary Whetsone of Victory Chistian Center in New Castle Deleware for the Impact his teachings has had on my life.

I was able to launch into ministry after sitting under him. I also would like to thank Apostle R.L. Jackson who's teaching and ministerial training I have been able to use up to the present day.

I would like to thank all who have given me the opportunity to teach and train in the Word of God from our former church in Coney Island Brooklyn "Victory International Christian Fellowship"

And our Present church Kingdom Manna International Church.

My present Executive Leadership team the Soto Family, the Myers Family, and the Weir Family. You'll have no idea the love I have for you.

I want to thank my father and mother and my brothers and their families for all of your love and support in all these years of life and Ministry.

Lastly, I would like to thank all of my sons and daughters starting with Isaiah, Christian, and Isaac to my daughters Destiny and Grace. My biggest supporter of all has been my precious wife Makita, who without your encouragement and support I would never completed this book. You have remained strong through all the storms of life it is now time for the Son to Shine through us. Thank you JESUS!!!!

TABLE OF CONTENTS

CHAPTER 1

THE SCEPTER OF
THE KINGDOM

ESTHER 5:1-3 "NOW *it came to pass on the third day, that Esther put on her royal apparel, and stood in the inner court of the king's house, over against the king's house: and the king sat upon his royal throne in the royal house, over against the gate of the house. And it was so, when the king saw Esther the queen standing in the court, that she obtained favor in his sight: and the king held out to Esther the golden scepter that was in his hand. So Esther drew near, and touched the top of the scepter. Then said the king unto her, what is thy request? It shall be even given thee to the half of the kingdom.*"

During the reign of King Ahasareus who reined from India to Ethiopia over one hundred and twenty seven provinces the King established a law in his kingdom. The law states according to Esther Chapter 4:11 *"that whosoever, whether man or woman, shall come unto the King into the inner court, who is not called, there is one law of his to put him to death, except such to whom the king shall hold out the golden scepter, that he may live: but I have not been called to come in unto the king these thirty days."*

As of recent years much has been discussed by way of preaching, bible studies and even the famous movie one night with the king as it concerns the book of Esther. Esther's main assignment was to petition the King on behalf of her people. The problem was a person could never state their petition before the king without being invited before the King. Esther decides to risk her own life to try to appear before the King without an invite, she declared "If I perish than I perish." There is nothing like a made up mind but even more powerful is when your will is submitted to the will of God. Esther realizes after hiding her identity that she became queen for such a time as this.

God strategically positions His people so that His purposes are re-alized in the earth. It was the favor of God and man that caused Esther to become queen, now she must petition the king on behalf of her people. Nothing can replace favor in a person's life. The favor of God upon your life will cause things to happen that don't normally hap-pen. Doors will open for you that only favor can open. Many times God places His favor upon the lives of those who have many obstacles against them. One day of favor can do more for you than years of your own labor. Favor will cause you to be supernaturally positioned for im-pact like Esther was. It's time for you to impact this generation because of favor on your life. Because of favor King Ahasareus extended the golden scepter Esther's way and gave her an invitation to enter into his presence to state her request. Esther Chapter 3 states that the king held out the golden scepter in his hand and Esther touched the top of the scepter. Just what was this golden scepter and what did it symbolize?

In my study of kings and queens these types of governmental structures were referred to as monarchies. A monarchy is a form of government in which total sovereignty is invested in one person, a head of state called a monarch, who holds the position until death or abdication. Monarchs usually both hold and achieve their position through the right of hereditary succession, they were related, usually the son or daughter, of the previous monarch. Notice that a monarch is usually born into it. The king in a monarch possessed an item referred to as a scepter usually looking like a rod or a staff. It symbolized sovereignty, royal authority or the dominion of a monarch. It symbolized power and with it kings usually sovereignly legislated law.

Where the word of a king is there is power. As Esther enters the presence of her king she touches the top of the staff symbolizing she is in right standing with the king. To be in right standing with the king meant she was obeying the law of her king and now the king was ready to legislate for her. To be in right standing with the king meant to be righteous. In many religious circles, including Christianity, righteous is used as a religious term but in a kingdom type government it is a legal term meaning right standing or law abiding. There is no way to be in right standing with the king without keeping his law.

In the beginning of the book of Esther King Ahasareus had another queen by the name of Vashti. The king commanded for her to be called during a royal celebration so he could show off her beauty but she refused to come. In other words she was unrighteous because she didn't keep the king's command. As a result of this she was removed from being queen and stripped of her authority while Esther became her replacement. Esther was someone who would keep herself in right standing. Because she was righteous she was granted access to enter into the king's presence.

In verse 3 of chapter 5 she's asked what her request is and is told it shall be given thee to the half of the kingdom. In Luke's gospel chapter 12 verses 31-32 we are told to seek the kingdom of God because it is the Father's good pleasure to give us the kingdom. In Matthew 6:35 it says *"But seek ye first the kingdom of God, and his righteousness: and all these things shall be added unto you."* We are not only encouraged to seek for the rule and reign of God (the kingdom) but also His righteousness. Not our righteousness but his righteousness. What does righteousness have to do with the kingdom?"

I hope you are ready for your life to take on a whole new level of understanding. With every new level of understanding you are to impact more of your generation. Are you ready to live a life that really matters? In Hebrews 1:8-9 it says *"But unto the son he saith, thy throne, O God, is for ever and ever: a scepter of righteousness is the scepter of thy kingdom. Thou hast loved righteousness, and hated iniquity; therefore God, even thy God hath anointed thee with the oil of gladness above thy fellows."* In this scripture we are told the throne of the Lord Jesus is eternal, He is King forever and ever. The Kingdoms of this world are become the Kingdoms of our Lord, and of His Christ; and He shall reign forever and ever. (Revelation 11:15)

CHAPTER 2

CHRIST THE KING

JESUS IS REFERRED to as the Christ. Christ is not Jesus' last name it is His eternal title. Christ means the Messiah and it also means the anointed one. If He is the anointed one He must be anointed for a purpose. As we read Psalms 2 in the Bible we are taught that He is anointed to be King. In Isaiah chapter 9:6-7, it says *"For unto us a child is born, unto us a son is given: and the government shall be upon his shoulder: and his name shall be called Wonderful, Counselor, The Mighty God, The Everlasting Father, The Prince of Peace. Of the increase of His government and peace there shall be no end, upon the throne of David, and upon his Kingdom, to order it, and to establish it with judgment and with justice from henceforth-even forever. The zeal of the Lord of hosts will perform this."* This scripture reveals that none other but the incarnate Christ came to the earth in order to restore the government of God into the earth realm.

This process began by the reconciling of man to God the original rulers in the earth whose assignment was to establish the kingdom of heaven in the earth realm. Christ came to redeem man back to God and restore mankind to their original purpose. Unless a man is born again he cannot perceive the Kingdom of God. When Adam and Eve fell they lost the dominion they received from the Father, the moment they lost the God image, they lost their dominion.

Jesus came to restore to man the ability to use the scepter again. Jesus is the king but he made us kings, He is the Lord but he has made us lords. Remember a scepter has a rod used by a king that symbolizes power and authority. In Hebrews 1:8 we are taught the scepter of God's son is a scepter of righteousness. This means that the Kingdom Jesus is King over is a kingdom in which the throne of the king is established in righteousness. In this kingdom in order to operate in kingdom authority righteousness is the foundation. Righteousness is a legal term and not a religious one. To be righteous means to be in right standing or rightly positioned. If the law of the king or the word of the king is not kept you are not righteous because you are not in right standing. To be righteous means you keep the law.

When Esther came into the presence of King Ahasareus he extended his golden scepter her way. She enters his presence and touches the top of the scepter signifying she was in right standing with the king. The former queen, Vashti, whom Esther replaced, lost her position because she was unrighteous. She didn't keep the law or word of the King. During a royal celebration in Esther chapter one, he commanded for Vashti to be brought before him and his guests to show off her beauty, but Vashti refused to come.

What a King says is not a matter of suggestion; it is a command that demands obedience. When Vashti refused to come she lost her standing with the king, and another took her royal position. Vashti was brought into the presence of the king to be told she would never enter his presence again because she was unrighteous.

How was she unrighteous? Well because she refused to obey the word of her King it put her in a position where she could not enjoy the benefits of living in King Ahasareus' Kingdom.

Kingdom authority is given to those that obey the law of the king. Understanding the kingdom is critical because Colossians 1:13 says: "who hath delivered us from the power or dominion of darkness, and hath translated us into the kingdom of his dear Son. Darkness or the kingdom of darkness no longer has dominion over us because we serve a new King his name is Jesus. Notice we are right now in the kingdom of God's dear son. Remember when Adam sinned he lost dominion or kingdom; he no longer had the God image so he was stripped of complete authority in the earth. Jesus came to give us back our righteousness or right standing with the Father by giving us back the God image referred to as the fruit of the spirit in the New Testament.

The fruit of the spirit is the God image, which restores to us authority over the Devil and all his works. In the gospel of

Luke 17:19-20 Jesus said: "Behold I give unto you power (authority) to tread on serpents and scorpions and over all the power of the enemy; and nothing shall by any means hurt you. Not withstanding to this rejoice not, that the spirits are subject unto you; but rather rejoice, because your names are written in heaven."

According to these verses Jesus has given us authority over the power of the Devil. You don't fight power with power you fight power with authority. Authority gives us the legal right to use power. In order to have authority over Satan you must be submitted to God, the Word of God and God's delegated authority. Satan has power but he doesn't have authority. To have power without authority makes the usage of power illegal. Everything Satan does is illegal; he depends on our ignorance and his ability to deceive. The Word says that Jesus has made evil spirits to be subject unto us because we have authority. What gives us our authority?

Verse 20 is very important we are told not to rejoice because spirits are subject unto us but to rejoice because our names are written in heaven. This is telling us we are registered citizens of the Kingdom of heaven; our citizenship entitles us to kingdom authority. This authority is placed into the hands of those that are righteous, in right standing with the King. This next verse is the key to understanding this concept.

In Matthews's gospel Chapter 16:13-18 Jesus asks his disciples one of the key questions to being able to enter into the kingdom. In verse 13 Jesus asks his disciples whom do men say that I am? They responded by saying some say you are John the Baptist, some say you are Elijah and others Jeremiah or one of the prophets. They believed Jesus was one of these prophets reincarnated. In other words he was a great former prophet come back in another form. This understanding seeks to sabotage our uniqueness, "you were born for such a time as this." There has never been a you and there will never be another you, God has manifested you now so that you can impact your generation according to the will of God for your life. In verse 15 he asks one of the most important questions on which are the foundation of the Kingdom of God. He asks his disciples: *whom do you say that I am?* Peter answers and declares that he is the Christ the Son of the living God.

Remember earlier we discovered that the Christ wasn't his last name Jesus is the Christ. The Christ means not just Messiah but King! Not only is Jesus the Lamb of God but also He is the lion of the tribe of Judah. He IS KING HALLELUJAH!! He is not just Savior but He is also King. No one made him King He was not voted into power He was born King. Jesus responds to Peter and tells him that the source of his understanding not finds its origin in humanity but the Father revealed it unto him. In other words who Jesus was had to come from a realm of revelation knowledge not common knowledge. Notice before Jesus called him Simon Peter but after Simon Peter's declaration Jesus said, "You are Peter." The name Simon means unstable or shaky but the moment he declared who Jesus was he was now called Peter, a rock or stable. Jesus declares that upon this revelation He would build his church and the gates of hell shall not prevail against it.

CHAPTER 3

———— ✦ ————

UNIFORMITY OR UNITY

FOR TOO LONG we've been building the church on Jesus being savior. You enter the church upon Jesus being savior but you build the church upon Christ being King. Whatever a king speaks is law, kings issue decrees. It's impossible to be in right standing with the king if you don't do what he says. As citizens of the kingdom of Gods dear son we must obey the words of our king. We don't sit at round table discussions to see if his word is relevant for this generation we obey the word of our king. Satan's job is to deceive us so our authority over him and his kingdom are limited, because our disobedience affects our authority. The word of Gods says in the book of James 4:7 *"Submit you therefore to God, Resist the devil and he will flee from you."* Jesus goes on to explain that he would give the keys of the kingdom of heaven to the church and he says whatever we bind on earth must be what's bound in heaven and whatever we loose on earth shall be what's loosed in heaven. While the church has just been focused on getting people to heaven these verses reveal that we are called to completely impact society. We are supposed to affect change so strongly in the world that we make it a struggle for Satan to easily capture a generation. The church has made it easier for Satan because we are not operating on the level of kingdom authority that Jesus has delegated unto us. When Jesus said whatever we bind he was talking about whatever we don't permit, lock up or declare unlawful. Then to loose is to permit, unlock or declare lawful. To the church his called out ones has been given this authority, which we have not been using. As a result of not understanding the keys Satan has gained access into the areas that he has no authority to rule. Our assignment has been to get as many to heaven as possible with forgetting that we must affect this world's system on the earth in order to deliver people out of the world's system.

We've been going to the world instead of going into the entire world. In whatever part of this worlds system where there are people in darkness we must go into it as the church to rescue them. You may go in as a lawyer, doctor, athlete, teacher, dentist, astronaut, accountant, manager, etc. The assignment is to reconcile man to God we've been given the keys of the kingdom of heaven by using the right key or principle we can cause God's system to manifest right in the world. It's time for the sons of God to come forth and cause a shifting to entire systems. If we don't like the things going on in the world then we must use the keys of the kingdom of heaven to bring change. In Matthew chapter 18 Jesus shares this same concept again but he goes a little further in its understanding.

Matthew 18:18-20 says "verily I say unto you, whatsoever ye shall bind on earth shall be bound in heaven: and whatsoever ye shall loose on earth shall be loosed in heaven. Again I say unto you, that if two of you shall agree on earth as touching anything that they shall ask, it shall be done for them of my Father, which is in heaven. For where two or three are gathered together in my name, there am I in the midst of them."

These are some very powerful verses they reveal to us why the church's authority is compromised in society. Jesus said that if any two shall agree. So the power to bind and loose is at its greatest when the church can agree on earth or get in agreement. The church has been diluted of its authority as we have raised up our own disciples instead of Disciples of Christ. Many well meaning men and women in the church have separated themselves from other parts of the body weakening our power to this generation. Many of us have not learned the difference between unity and uniformity. You can be uniform and not be united. Our unity must be as a result of our diversity understanding as we come together we form one body in Christ.

Another way to look at unity God's way understands a symphony. A symphony is composed of many different instruments but they unite under a composer that causes them to play the same song in harmony. True unity is when we don't over emphasize parts of the body or try to outdo each other; unity results where there is harmony. There is no unity without the church having the same mission but different ways of fulfilling that mission. We can't walk together unless we are in agreement concerning where we are going. The mission of the church simply put is to reconcile man to god. There are varied ways this is accomplished. Our gifts are given to fulfill our mission, which is the same. Our gifts may be different but our mission is the same. How can we ever walk in kingdom authority divided following men and not God? For many have gone establishing their own kingdom and not God's. According to Psalm 133 where there is unity God commands the blessing. This is the time where the church must come together in all its variety to form one awesome body in the Lord. No more body parts claiming separatism from the rest of the body. Many churches and ministries have made the mistake of building after their particular gifting instead of building according to the pattern in the word of God.

Our agreement in the earth must be what's already agreed upon in heaven and we will see it manifest in the earth. We must be about heavens agenda in the earth. Remember thy kingdom come thy will be done in earth as it is in heaven. Our love for God and each other will make it possible to be one. The world system is supposed to know who our king is based upon the love we have for each other. Our love for each other is supposed to be the catalyst that causes incredible unity. When we become one it will cause the Father to go to work bringing to pass his every desire for the territory called earth. In the days ahead we will see more of what's in heaven operating in and through the church on earth. In Revelation Chapter 5 before the throne of God worshipping, there were people from every kindred, and language, and people, and nation. There was a multi-cultural, multi-ethnic representation. These exact kinds of churches will be manifested in the earth operating with kingdom authority. It's only mature sons that the Father releases kingdom authority to. Once the church in earth begins to look like heaven we will become a mighty force in the earth. As of now, we are not walking in complete authority because we are ignorant of the righteousness of God.

In Romans chapter 10:1-3 it says

"Brethren, my hearts desire and prayer to God for Israel is that they might be saved. For me bear they record that they have zeal of God, but not according to knowledge. For them being ignorant of God's righteousness, and going about to establish their own righteousness, have not submitted them unto the righteousness of God."

The emphasis in this scripture is the nation of Israel but this can apply to any religious activity outside of walking in the righteousness of God. There are many who have a zeal for God and it's led to a religious experience wherein rules are followed in order to be righteous before God. You can be zealous for God but get the wrong knowledge. Our zeal for God must not end in joining a religion it should cause us to ask God to reveal himself. It will lead you into a personal relationship, not some religious experience.

Satan, himself, hides behind the kingdom of religion. The bible never identifies the first Adam with a religion he was simply called

God's son. The last Adam (Jesus) was never identified with a religion he was also called God's son. It's very possible for the light (religion) that people have really been darkness. We don't need our own righteousness. We need the righteousness of God. Without righteousness we can't operate in kingdom authority. The scepter of the kingdom is righteousness. So without the revelation of righteousness our authority is limited. Satan knows in order for the church to have victory over his works we need authority but without righteousness our authority is very limited. How do we receive the righteousness of God?

The righteousness of God is received by grace through faith. In other words there is nothing that we can do in our own ability to be called the righteousness of God. We receive it by receiving God's free gift of salvation made possible by Jesus. A powerful scripture to help us understand this concept is II Corinthians 5:21 it says: *"For he hath made him to be sin for us, who knew no sin that we might be made the righteousness of God in him."* Another understanding of this scripture is that God took the sinless Christ and poured upon him our sins at the cross and then God took the righteousness of Christ and made it available to man upon receiving salvation. The righteousness of Christ is a gift to be received by faith. The book of Romans chapter 5:19 teaches us *"For as by one mans (Adam's) disobedience many were made sinners, so by the obedience of one shall many be made righteous."* What a powerful scripture Adam sinned and sin had dominion over us, Jesus paid the price for sin and obeyed the Father and now righteousness has caused us to receive our dominion back again. We no longer have to be slaves to sin we are to live as sons of God. In verse 17 of Romans 5 righteousness is called a gift. What do you do with a gift? You receive it, unwrap it and enjoy it. Remember to be righteous means to be rightly positioned; you now have access to petition the king. This gift of righteousness makes you a very powerful individual because you have access to the king. You can come before the king and petition him concerning his desires. I John 5:14-15 says: *"And this is the confidence that we have in him that, if we ask anything according to his will he heareth us: and if we know that he hears us, whatsoever we ask, we know that we have the petitions that we desired of him."* When we pray according to the will of God our petitions are granted. Not my will but your will be done, Hallelujah.

CHAPTER 4

∼✦∼

THE POWER OF RIGHTEOUSNESS

THE SCEPTER OF the kingdom is a scepter of righteousness. Everything concerning the kingdom of God is righteousness; God's throne is established upon righteousness. When you operate in righteousness you do right because it is right. The kingdom of God consists of righteousness, peace and joy in the Holy Spirit. There is no peace and joy without righteousness. Please be reminded when we talk about righteousness being received by faith we are talking about the very righteousness of Christ. The same righteousness he operated in when he was tempted in Luke 4 just like the first Adam and passed the test. He was tempted with the lust of the flesh, the lust of the eyes and pride of life but prevailed because of righteousness. When in the garden of Gethsemane he declared not my will but thine be done and remained righteous. When the innocent suffered for the guilt and he declared *"Father into thine hand I commit my spirit."* When the third day after his death came he was raised from the dead because of righteousness. This is the righteousness we receive upon receiving Jesus as Lord. This is not trying to do things to be righteous; this is being righteous and then doing the works of righteousness. Again, righteousness is a gift made available upon receiving salvation.

This next statement though is so controversial but yet so true. WE ARE NOT SINNERS SAVED BY GRACE! WE ARE THE RIGHTEOUSNESS OF GOD IN CHRIST. To be sinners would mean Jesus did not undo the work of the first Adam. Remember through one man's disobedience many were made sinners, through one man's obedience shall many be made righteous. The most important thing we need to do upon receiving salvation is not to be conformed to this world's system but to be transformed by the renewing of our mind. All of our thought patterns shaped by operating in this world's system must change by having our thought patterns changed by the word of god. We must learn to think like the new us and not the old us. Our main struggle is in the mind, when our minds are free we are free. As we allow God's word to strip off our old thought patterns and we begin to develop new thought patters we are gradually transformed into the image of Christ in the word of God, as we go from glory to glory. What happens to our righteousness when we sin?

I John 1:9 say *"If we confess our sins, he is faithful and just to forgive us our sins, and to cleanse us from all unrighteousness."* When Jesus suffered for sin he paid the price for sinners past, present and future. This gives us no license to sin the grace of God is more than unmerited favor it is also the ability to do what we could never do without grace. Our great Father as we ask provides for us the grace to overcome habits, repetitive sins, iniquity in our family line and whatever else could try to overcome us. We are over comers in Christ. Thank God that the blood of Jesus cleanses us from everything not in conformity to God's will and purpose, thought and action. The diabolical plan of the enemy is to come against our authority by attacking our righteousness.

Have you noticed yet a major increase in wickedness in our society?

Sin has become more readily accessible than it's ever been. What is the kingdom of darkness after? Satan is after the righteousness of the saints, he desires to move us out of position so that we become law breakers and even worse lawless. The spirit of lawlessness is becoming stronger in our generation where people no longer have a regard for what's right; it's every man for himself. Paul the apostle declared that a spirit of lawlessness would be prevalent in the last days. What this generation so desperately needs are people who will keep the law of God and operate in righteousness.

God has been known to hold back judgment because of the righteous. In many instances in the Old Testament God said he would spare a whole city if he could find just a few people walking in righteousness. People who walk in righteousness in the midst of a corrupt society become valuable to God. The righteous have a have a special place in God's heart. When the earth became corrupt in the days of a man by the name of Noah in Genesis God judged the people on earth by way of a flood. God began again with Noah and his family they were told to repopulate the earth again. God chose Noah because he was righteous. We need true sons of God to be planted in every realm of society to manifest the righteousness of God. Righteousness exalts a nation but sin causes a nation to be destroyed. God will exalt the nation because of the righteous. Remember, you can never be made righteous without receiving the righteousness of God given as a gift once Jesus becomes your Lord.

Satan is well aware of the truth that the keys of the kingdom have been given to the righteous. He uses every method possible to affect your consciousness of the righteousness of God. He uses the kingdoms of this world to preoccupy your mind and your time so that you don't walk in righteousness. Righteousness is a gift, but what good is a gift that is never unwrapped. You must learn all you can of the righteousness of God so you can walk in it. If you live with a sin consciousness instead of a righteousness consciousness you will sin instead of doing the works of righteousness. Whatever you meditate on the most is what you will produce. As a man thinks in his heart so is he.

In I John Chapter 2:29 it says that the person that doeth righteousness is born of God. Those who have experienced the new birth are supposed to be a people walking in righteousness. Those who don't do righteousness are not of God. How do we do righteousness when there are struggles we battle inside of us and outside of us? We must walk in the spirit so that we don't fulfill the lust of the flesh. Instead of trying not to fulfill the lusts of the flesh our focus must be on walking in the spirit. If we successfully walk in the spirit we will not have any problems with the flesh. We will have battles and struggles but we must learn how to pray so we can receive power from God to resist the urges of the flesh. Jesus said as we pray we will not enter into temptation. The flesh is weak but the spirit is willing. Our victory comes as we do things to build strength in our spirit. As long as our spirit continues to feed on the things of God we walk in victory over the flesh. The moment we feed the flesh more than we do our spirit we begin to struggle with the flesh. Instead of focusing on not doing wrong we must focus on doing right and we will be victorious. Remember kingdom authority is released to those who walk in righteousness, do everything possible to walk in authority. When you walk in authority you experience the benefits of righteousness.

In the bible it is very clear that those who walk in righteousness have a special place in the kingdom of God. To walk in righteousness means you walk with God because He is a righteous god. One of the first benefits of walking in righteousness is you have access to the king (God). The prayer of a righteous person is powerful because it's heard. People who walk in righteousness can actually come before the king whenever necessary. When Esther was to appear before King Ahasareus in Esther Chapter 5 she put on her royal apparel. Well our king has also given us royal apparel as his children it is called the robe of righteousness. In Isaiah 61:10 says "*I will greatly rejoice in the Lord, my soul shall be joyful in my God; for he hath clothed me with the garments of salvation, he hath covered me with the robe of righteousness, as a bridegroom decketh himself with ornaments, and as a bride adorneth herself with her jewels."* Notice this scripture says the moment we receive salvation God gives us a robe of righteousness. You don't do righteousness and then are called righteous. God calls you righteous after you receive the gift of salvation then you do the works of righteousness. Remember righteousness puts you in position with the king you receive the benefits of a citizen who keeps the law. Psalms 103:2 say

"Forget not all his benefits." There are tremendous benefits to walking in righteousness. The word says in Psalms 103 that God *"forgives all iniquities, he heals all diseases, he redeems our lives from destruction, he crowns us with loving kindness and tender mercies. He satisfies our mouths with good things; so that our youth is renewed like the eagles."*

One of the most powerful stories in the bible revealing the power the righteous have with God is in Genesis Chapter 18:16-33. In the beginning of the chapter Abraham and Sarah entertain three visitors who were actually angels. As they are about to leave and head towards Sodom and Gomorrah the visitation gets more powerful. The Lord in verses 17-19 says *"And the Lord said, shall I hide from Abraham that thing which I do: seeing that Abraham shall surely become a great and mighty nation, and all the nations of the earth shall be blessed in him? For I know him, that he will command his children and his household after him, and they shall keep the way of the Lord, to do justice and judgment, that the Lord may bring upon Abraham that which he hath spoken of him."* God reveals some of his future plans to the righteous walking in righteousness will cause you to walk in a realm of revelation. The Lord reveals his purpose for choosing Abraham. Abraham would command his children and grandchildren to walk in righteousness so God could fulfill his word to his generations. The generation of the upright shall be blessed Hallelujah!

CHAPTER 5

RIGHTEOUSNESS WILL PRESERVE A NATION

WALKING IN UNRIGHTEOUSNESS brings you out of right position with God you can't walk in his benefits. Righteous people walk in kingdom authority; notice the scripture said that Abraham would command his children. We need more Abrahams today, people who will command their seed to serve God and they become the example. This generation is in need of seeing people who walk upright before God and are blessed as a result of right living. In the next few verses the Lord prepares to go and see if Sodom and Gomorrah is as grievous as the sound of their sin ascending into the heavens. In verse 23 Abraham asks the Lord a life-changing question: *"Will you destroy the righteous with the wicked?"* Listen to what Abraham says to the Lord in verses 24 – 25

"Per adventure there is fifty righteous within the city: will you also destroy and not spare the place for the fifty righteous that are therein? That be far from thee to do after this manner, to slay the righteous with the wicked: and that the righteous should be as the wicked, that is far from thee: Shall

not the Judge of all the earth do right?" Abraham had a revelation of the righteousness of God. Righteous people do what's right because it is right. The Lord's response to Abraham is powerful he says if he can find fifty righteous people in the city for the sake of the fifty he will not destroy the city. How awesome, the righteouses are that important to society that they can cause judgment to be held back. Satan in his nature is a destroyer and has a desire to see people destroyed; this is why he hates the righteous. The righteouses have power with God and we know there is nothing impossible with God. In this generation we are in the battle that is intensifying for the souls of humanity. However I declare to you that God has a remnant that will not bow to the spirit of compromise in our generation. This righteous remnant will be responsible for one of the greatest moves of God's spirit to ever be experienced. This righteous remnant will be the catalyst for what our God is about to do in the earth. This righteous remnant will be the salt of the earth; this righteous remnant will cause the move of God's Spirit to be released in many of our cities and nations in America and around the world.

Abraham started off asking God if he would preserve the city for the sake of fifty righteous people. The amazing thing concerning Abraham's intercession is he goes from 50 – 45 and the Lord gives him the same response. He then goes from 45 – 40 and the Lord says for the sake of the 40 he would preserve the city. Abraham continues this same intercession until he gets all the way down to ten and the answer is the same for the sake of the ten. The Lord promises he would not destroy Sodom and Gomorrah. This is an amazing exchange between the Lord and Abraham and it shows us the power of righteousness. The righteous has significant favor and power with God.

The righteous is truly the salt in the earth. Salt is used for flavor and it is also used to preserve things. The righteous will cause a city and a nation to be preserved. If we ever needed people that walk in the revelation of righteousness with the scepter of the kingdom in their grasp, it is now.

CHAPTER 6

THE REVELATION OF RIGHTEOUSNESS

As we discussed earlier, according to 2Corinthians 5:21 *"He who knew no sin was made to be sin for us that we might be made the righteousness of God in Christ."* Please remember this righteousness we are discussing here that causes one to walk in the authority of the kingdom is a gift. I pray you are somewhere sitting or relaxing so you can truly grasp this truth I am about to share with you on righteousness. In Romans chapter five we are given an amazing teaching on justification by faith.

When we speak of justification we are referring to Gods act of declaring those guilty of sin and offending his holy nature as not guilty. You heard correctly because of the sinless dying for the sinful we through faith in Jesus, are declared not guilty and also have been given right standing with the Father. Romans 5:1 let us know because we are justified by faith (not works), we have peace with God through our Lord Jesus Christ. Did you know God is not angry with you His son made reconciliation with the Father possible? Not only have we been reconciled we also have access. Remember Queen Esther was granted access by the king as he extended his golden scepter towards her. Well we also have access to the Father because we have been granted favor through being justified by faith. To be justified means just as if it never was, Jesus paid for our sins at the cross past, present and future. He freed us from sin, and the devil even again having dominion over us. In other words we don't have to yield to sin anymore. Sin has lost its dominion over us. A true believer with revelation of redemption will never again come under sins dominion. We are to no longer be slaves to sin but slaves to righteousness, glory! This stuff is awesome news but lets get to what the Holy Spirit really wants to show us.

In Romans 5:12 it says, *"Wherefore, as by one man sin entered into the world, and death by sin; and so death passed upon all men, for that all have sinned."* In the Amplified Bible it says it this way, "therefore as sin came into the world through one man, and death as the result of sin, so death spread to all men, (no one being able to stop it or to escape its power) because all men sinned. Beloved what this is actually saying to us is when God created the first man Adam and he sinned one time, his sin affected the whole human race. When he sinned he sold the whole human race into sin. You see when God first formed his body from the dust and breathed into his nostrils the breath of life God never had to go to the dust again to make another person. Everyone to ever be born in the earth was in the first man Adam in seed form. Did you and I ever eat of the fruit of the tree? Did we sin after the likeness of Adam? Of course not but we were in Adam and all we had to do in order to be directly affected by his disobedience is be born. The moment we are born into the earth the disobedience of our forefather Adam has a direct affect on us. We never have to be taught to sin because we are born into sin and shaped in iniquity, simply because of his disobedience. Now listen to what I am about to say, "If you never did anything to be born a sinner then what makes you think you have to do anything to be made the righteousness of God?" What did you ever do to be born a sinner? Nothing at all just be born!

Well how do we become the righteousness of God in Christ? Are you ready to praise this amazing God that we serve? In Romans 5:15-16 it states and I summarize, that Adams one transgression led to condemnation, which is the guilt of doing wrong along with the punishment connected to it. However, it states that God's free gift is of many offences unto justification, Hallelujah!! This means that the first Adam messed up one time and it resulted in judgment but the last Adam Jesus suffered for many sins and the many transgressions we have committed has led to justification.

Since the sinless Jesus has paid the price for our redemption we can now receive the abundance of grace and God's free gift of righteousness. I Corinthians 15:45 refer to Jesus as the last Adam who restores the dead back to life. Think of it this way, in order to be negatively affected by the first Adams disobedience all we had to do was be born. Well in order to be positively affected by the last Adam's obedience all we need to do is be born again. The moment we are born again we receive the abundance of grace and gift of righteousness. This gift of righteousness is not given based upon us earning it or deserving it, we receive it when we are born again. The New birth is God's answer to the sin problem. If we did nothing to be born a sinner we can do nothing to become righteous.

In review, when the first Adam disobeyed, we were sold into sin. The moment we are born, we are born into sin and shapened in iniquity. Well the last Adam reversed it all because he paid the price for sins and resurrected because of him being sinless. The moment we are born again we are birthed into victory because he defeated sin and loved righteousness. He hated iniquity so we receive God's abundant grace for the sins his son has already paid for and we receive God's free gift of righteousness. We are righteous because of Jesus and all we need to do is be born again. His righteousness becomes our righteousness. Just take a moment to pause and give Him praise; Jesus deserves it!

Now you can fully understand what Paul was saying about Israel in Romans 10:1-4. Paul says, *"Brethren my heart's desire and prayer to God for Israel is, that they might be saved. For I bear them record that they have zeal of God, but not according to knowledge. For they being ignorant of God's righteousness, and going about to establish their own righteousness, have not submitted themselves unto the righteousness of God. For Christ is the end of the law for righteousness to every one that believeth."* Family in these scriptures we have the definition of religion. There are many people that have great zeal and enthusiasm for God but their trust is in their own works. They argue about what clothing to wear or not wear. They argue about how to wear their hair, should one have a bread and so forth and so on. Sadly, much of the trouble in the world today, including war is all in the name of religion. What Paul declares is many have zeal for God but not according to the correct knowledge. Unfortunately, they don't understand the gospel. They have established their own righteousness but have not submitted to God's righteousness. If they only knew the answer is unless a man be born again he cannot inherit the kingdom of God. The answer is the new birth. Why struggle to be right before God keeping the law when Jesus came to fulfill all of its types and shadows. Would you rather a shadow of God or God himself? Would you rather hug your family members shadow or the real person.

Jesus is the real deal when you receive him the gather can now make available to you everything he desires to because of the obedience of the last Adam. If God the Father spared not his only Son, but delivered him up for us all, how shall he not through that same son freely give us all things? If you try to work for it then you have to earn it. However, why try to earn what Jesus has made available to you, not for your earning it or deserving it but receiving the last Adam as your Lord and Savior and his victory becoming your victory.

In Ephesians 2:8 it says, *"For you are saved by grace through faith and thus not of yourselves it is the gift of God, not of works lest any man can boast."* People are working so hard to be righteous before God that they have not submitted themselves to the righteousness of God. God has made a way to be righteous before him and his name is Jesus. He is the way the truth and the life, no man can come to the Father except they come through him. He is the last Adam and represents everything we shall become.

CHAPTER 7

───※───

ESTABLISHED IN
RIGHTEOUSNESS

WHEN WE RECEIVE Him as our Lord and Savior we are saved by grace and we receive the gift of righteousness. In Romans 4:25 we are told *"who was delivered for our offences, and was raised again for our justification."* This means he was put to death in the flesh because of our offences, but is resurrection from the dead is proof to us that any man that receives him as our sin substitute receives justification. God has removed our sins as far as the east from the west. God through his son has broken sin's dominion, we must believe the goodness of the gospel and submit to the righteousness of God.

Why is it so important to receive this righteousness that comes by way of a gift? This righteousness is the very righteousness that Jesus walked in his earth walk. Romans 1:16-17 says, *"For I am not ashamed of the gospel of Christ: for it is the power of God unto salvation to everyone that believeth, to the Jew first, and also to the Greek. For therein is the righteousness of God revealed from faith to faith: as it is written, the just shall live by faith.* "Notice in this scripture we are told there is a righteousness of God revealed from faith to faith.

We must understand that Paul declares the gospel he preached did not come from man's teaching, it to him, came by way of the revelation of Jesus Christ. It was given to him by the Holy Spirit in Galatians 1:11-12. Paul grew up as a religious man being a part of a group called the Pharisees. After being saved, Paul went everywhere declaring that no longer did Jewish laws have to be obeyed to be right in God's sight, that faith in Jesus Christ makes a man righteous in God's sight. Paul was greatly persecuted by the religious people of his day for preaching righteousness by faith.

Notice in Romans 10:4 we are told that Christ is the end of the law for righteousness to everyone that believeth. In Romans 3:22 it says, *"Even the righteousness of God which is by faith of Jesus Christ unto all and upon all them that believe: for there is no difference."* In Romans 3:26 it says, *"To declare, I say, at this time his righteousness: that he might be just, and the justifier of him which believeth in Jesus."*

If you want peace, quietness, and assurance it all comes as a result of righteousness. Listen to what Isaiah 32:15-20 says, *"until the spirit be poured upon us from on high, and the wilderness be a fruitful field, and the fruitful field be counted for a forest. Then judgment shall dwell in the wilderness and righteousness remain in the fruitful field. And the work of righteousness shall be peace; and the effect of righteousness, quietness and assurance forever. And my people shall dwell in peaceable habitation, and in sure dwellings, and in quiet resting places; and it shall hail, coming down on the forest; and the city shall be low in a low place. Blessed are ye that sow beside all waters that send for thither the feet of the ox and the donkey."*

From this scripture we are shown that one of the first results of righteousness would be peace. Verse one says the work of righteousness shall be peace. We are talking about the word for peace in Hebrew, which is "shalom." Shalom means completeness, soundness, welfare, and peace. It is translated also as success. In the book of Isaiah Chapter 54 God talks about his eternal covenant of peace. It says though the mountains be shaken and the hills be removed, yet my unfailing love for you will not be shaken nor my covenant of peace, says the Lord who has compassion on you. It also says all you children will be taught by the Lord, and great will be their peace. True shalom comes only from God because we are justified by faith we have peace with God. The blood of Jesus has turned us from being enemies of God by our wicked works to being sons of God. The work of righteousness produces shalom.

In addition to peace notice that righteousness also produces quietness and assurance, which is confidence. Confidence is very important because without it there will be difficulty in expecting God to do what he ways he will do. Righteousness produces confidence even in your prayers being answered. In 1 John 5:14 it says *"And this is the confidence that we have in him, that, if we ask anything according to his will he heareth us: and if we know that he hears us, whatsoever we ask, we know that we have the petitions that we desired of him."* That is very powerful to know that our confidence in God is strengthened through the gift of righteousness.

As we conclude this chapter on the revelation of righteousness I want to give just a couple more scriptures to further establish you in this revelation. Listen to Isaiah 54:14 *"In righteousness shall thou be established; thou shalt be far from oppression; for thou shall not fear and from terror, it shall not come near thee."* According to this scripture people that are oppressed need to be established in righteousness. Oppression is the exercise of power or authority in an unjust or cruel manner. In Acts 10:38 we are told how God anointed Jesus of Nazareth with the Holy Ghost and power who went about doing good healing all of those oppressed by the devil for God was with him. Satan and is realm oppress people but when you get established in righteousness you will be far from oppression. To get established in something means to become fixed or immovable in it. You are to meditate in the power of righteousness until you get established you become free from oppression. Notice also when you get established you will not operate in fear or terror it will not come near you. The revelation of righteousness will produce boldness in your life. You will overcome whatever life throws at you because of your boldness that is a direct result of being established in righteousness.

In Proverbs 28:1 it says, *the wicked flee when no man pursueth: but the righteous are bold as a lion.* I have always been fascinated with lions and how bold they are. The righteous are called to be bold as lions. The righteous are suppose to reign in life through Jesus Christ. This doesn't mean you wont have trouble, Psalm 34:19 says, *"Many are the tests, trials and troubles of the righteous but the Lord will deliver them out of them all."* There is nothing that can come against you as the righteous that God will not see you through. What test are you going through? What trial are you in? What trouble has come against you? The righteous comes out of them all Hallelujah!! Be confident in your God and his promises. Be bold when you pray, be bold when you praise the Lion of the Tribe of Judah, who lives inside of you. Fear nothing the devil and life brings your way. You are more than a conqueror through Christ. Rejoice in suffering, triumph in trouble, you are the righteous, let your heart be fixed trusting in God's love and his promises.

CHAPTER 8

THE POWER OF PRAYER

IN THE BOOK of James 5:13-18 it says, *"Is any among you afflicted? Let him pray. Is any merry? Let him sing psalms. Is any sick among you? Let him call for the elders of the church; and let them pray over him, anointing him with oil in the name of the Lord: And the prayer of faith shall save the sick, and the Lord shall raise him up, and if he have committed sins they shall be forgiven him. Confess your faults one to another, and pray one for another, that e may be healed. The effectual fervent prayer of a righteous man availeth much. Elias was a man subject to like passions as we are, and he prayed earnestly that it might not rain: and it rained not on the earth by the space of three years and six months. And he prayed again, and the heavens gave rain, and the earth brought forth her fruit."*

Before we discuss these verses lets go back to the story of Esther. Lets remember in Esther Chapter 5 the Queen on the third day puts on her royal apparel as she prepared herself to go before the king in his throne room to petition him on behalf of her people. When the king saw the queen standing in the royal court she obtained favor in his sight and the king held out to Esther the golden scepter that was in his hand and she drew near and touched the top of the scepter. Then the king said to her what do you want and what is your request? I will give it to you up to half of my kingdom. My God does this get me excited, Esther found favor, and we also have favor. Esther was able to approach the king; we also have access to our king. She did something we need to do in our generation, Esther petitioned the king. Saints of God there are different types of prayer and different things we are to do when we pray.

To petition means to make a specific request. Esther's request had to do with the preservation of her people as Haman had made a plot to wipe out the Jews. She petitioned the king, he granted her request and her people were preserved. Instead of her people being wiped out, the one who conspired against them, Haman, was wiped out. The whole understanding of righteousness was to build up to this point. As the righteous we have favor with God. Esther was able to petition the king and her intercession saved an entire nation.

The bible says in James, the prayer of a righteous man availeth much and shall be heard. Do you hear this people of God? Because we have received the gift of righteousness, we have access to the Throne Room. We can petition our great Father and see things shift in the earth realm. We have power to bind and loose, or lock and unlock. Righteousness gives us access into the throne room people of God. Without righteousness we have no authority in the Kingdom. That's why in Hebrews 1 we are told the scepter of the kingdom is a scepter of righteousness. Righteousness gives us access to the throne room and righteousness entitles us as ambassadors to carry out business for the king in the earth. According to Matthew 6:33 we are to seek first the kingdom and his righteousness. We are to be about kingdom business in the earth realm. We are living in a generation where Satan is fighting harder than ever for the souls of humanity. We need the righteous, those with access to the throne room to begin to make specific request, for cities, for countries, for families, for the world. It's time for the righteous to pray bold and big prayers. Prayers beyond praying for basic needs, but prayers that make much power available to shake nations. We are living in a very satanic generation under Luciferian doctrine. We need Esthers, we need Daniels, and we need Elijahs who will pray the type of prayers that will shake their generation. If Esther didn't pray, her entire generation, including family members, would have

perished. She was positioned in the kingdom to approach the king for such a time as this.

You have been born again and translated into the kingdom of God's dear son for such a time as this. The Father already planned your birth in this generation He already foreknew which generation you would impact. Now its time for you to pray big prayers for your generation that will change many lives. I can see that God is raising up a new generation that understand they are the righteous and they are ready for His house to become a living mobile house of prayer. People of God, our God do not dwell in temples made with hands; He dwells in the lives of those that have received the gift of righteousness. It's time to use our righteousness to go to the king and find his purposes for our generation so we can impact it as we work with our God to fulfill His righteous plan. When I refer to praying big prayers, I'm talking about praying in such a way that our prayers impact multitudes positively. If we are to see the will of God done in our generation then the righteous must realize that our prayers make tremendous power available. But I believe what's even better is in James 5:16 we are told when we pray for one another we will be healed or made whole. Child of God you must realize what you make happen for others our God makes happen for you. Then it lets us know that the continued focused prayer of a righteous man makes much power available. In verse 17 of James 5 it goes into an example of this type of prayer and uses Elijah the prophet of God as an example. It lets us know Elijah was a human being just like us with feelings, affections and emotions. The word says he prayed earnestly for it not to rain and it didn't rain for three and a half years. Can you imagine Elijah lived in a generation much like ours where there was Baal worship? The word Baal means, "lord." Baal was a fertility god who was believed to enable the earth to produce crops and people to produce children. Different regions worshipped Baal in different ways, and Baal proved to be a highly adaptable god.

Various locales emphasized one or another of his attributes and developed special "denominations" of Baalism. The Canaanites worshipped Baal as the sun god and as the storm god – he is usually depicted holding a lightning bolt – which defeated enemies and produced crops. Baal worship was rooted in sensuality and involved ritualistic prostitution in the temples. At times appeasing Baal required human sacrifice usually the firstborn of the one making the sacrifice (Jeremiah 19:5). The priests of Baal appealed to their god in rites of wild abandon, which included loud, ecstatic cries and self-inflicted injury (I Kings 18:28).

Before the nation of Israel entered the promised land God warned against worshipping Canaan's gods, Deuteronomy 6:14-15, but Israel turned to idolatry any way. I went into this information for this reason, Elijah prayed for no rain but why did he pray for no rain? In I Kings 17:1 Elijah tells Ahab there would be no rain until he says so. God gave his prophet a word and Elijah went into intense prayer to see the word birthed in his generation. God was read to deal with a generation wrapped up in paganism. The people of God instead of remaining faithful to the worship of Jehovah began to serve IDOLS led by their king Ahab and his wife Jezebel. Elijah being led by god was about to show the God he served controlled the rain not Baal. Can you imagine this righteous man's prayers affected his entire locale? We need modern day Elijah's that hear God's word then go into effectual fervent prayer until it happens. People of God with power not this version of church we have today. Not to be so critical but we are to be more than those that talk about God and give nice bible lessons. Where is the God of Elijah that answers by fire? This generation needs the demonstration of the power of God. The righteous has access to He who sits on the throne. It's time to pray big prayers so that our generation will know the God we serve, He is the only true and living God.

In verse 18 of James 5 it says that Elijah prayed again, and the heaven gave rain, and the earth brought forth her fruit. In

I Kings 18:41 Elijah tells Ahab to get thee up eat and drink for there is a sound of abundance of rain. What did Elijah do when he heard the sound? He goes to the top of Mt. Carmel and gets into intense focused prayer. As he goes into intense focused prayer there is nothing by way of indication that rain is coming. But he continues in prayer until there was a cloud the size of a man's hand. This is what James is talking about when he mentions the effectual fervent prayer. It's praying until the breakthrough comes. I like to refer to it as praying through. Paul says in Galatians 4:19 "My little children, of whom I travail in birth again until Christ be formed in you." What he was actually saying is before you received Christ I travailed in prayer for your hearts to be open to the gospel. Now that you are born again I'm travailing in prayer again until you mature in Christ where you go from being babes in Christ to mature in Christ. In Isaiah 66:7-9 it says "Before she travailed, she brought forth; before her pain came, she was delivered of a man child. Who hath heard such a thing? Who hath seen such things? Shall the earth be made to bring forth in one day? Or shall a nation be born at once? For as soon as Zion travailed, she brought forth her children. Shall I bring to the birth, and not cause it to bring forth? Saith the Lord: shall I cause to bring forth, and shut the womb? Saith thy God." We must like Elijah get in the birth position and travail until the word of God is made flesh. I believe we are in the generation of those that will hold god to His word and pray until changes comes to this generation. Church our Father is calling us back to the place of prayer. I believe the prayers of the righteous will prevail in this generation and make much power available. I believe we will witness one of the greatest displays of God's power in this generation that will come forth because of the prayers of the righteous for many generations. The appointed time has come its time for the righteous to petition the King!

CHAPTER 9

THE OIL OF JOY

IN THIS CHAPTER I want to share something with you that is a very important component of the gift of righteousness. In Hebrews 1:8-9 it says "But unto the Son He saith, thy throne, O God, is forever and ever: a scepter of righteousness is the scepter of thy kingdom. Thou hast loved righteousness, and hated iniquity; therefore God, even thy God, hath anointed thee with the oil of gladness above thy fellows." The amplified bible calls it the oil of joy and gladness. Notice what God promised to do for His son, He said because He loved righteousness and hated iniquity He was going to give him the oil of joy and gladness. There are three things that describe the kingdom of God; it is righteousness, peace and joy in the Holy Ghost. People of God whatever happened to being filled with joy. That joy you received when Jesus became your Lord and the heavy burden of sin was rolled away. I want to talk to you in this chapter about the oil of joy. Notice it was God that said He would anoint Jesus with the oil of joy and gladness. In Galatians chapter 5:22 when it mentions the fruit of the spirit the second thing mentioned in the list is joy. This oil of joy and gladness comes from God's Spirit. You may ask how? Well we all need to be challenged in our view of God. He is nothing like the picture religion paints of Him. He is full of joy and gladness. You heard correctly He is a joyful and glad God. The bible in Psalms 2 and other places even let's us know He laughs. That's right God laughs because He is full of life; He is full of joy and gladness. When you are God and all power is in your hand you can be full of joy and gladness. I don't know about you but with all the problems and trouble in this world I need the oil of joy and gladness. There are too many of God's people that are oppressed, we are presenting the wrong view of God to the world. In the book of Acts there was a man named Phillip who preached the gospel to the city of Samaria (Acts 8:4-8) it says, "Therefore they that were scattered abroad went everywhere preaching the word. Then Phillip went down to the city of Samaria, and preached Christ unto them. And the people with one accord gave heed unto those things which Phillip spake, hearing and seeing the miracles that he did. For unclean spirits, crying with loud voices, came out of many that were possessed with them: and many taken with palsies and that were lame, were healed. And there was great goy in that city." Why was there joy in that city? Because God was in that city. When God shows up joy shows up. The life full of joy and gladness is the righteous life not the life filled with sin and the things of the world. It's sad when we as believers say lets go have some fun and we associate fun with doing stuff outside of God's presence. Can I tell you there is a generation arising that will operate in the joy of the Lord? God says at His right hand are pleasures forever more. It also says in Revelation 4:11 that God created all things for His pleasure. Wow, that means we are created to please God. The miserable life is when we live to please ourselves and even others. The awesome life is when we live to please God. When we live to please Him He will give us the oil of joy and gladness.

Do you know how many people are unhappy and miserable so they go from one thing to the next? From one job to the next from one partner to the next partner they try drugs, alcohol, pop pills looking for joy and gladness. And that joy and gladness only comes when you begin to live for the one who created you for his good pleasure. There is great joy and peace living for the one who created you for his good pleasure. Instead of living to gain things, living for people, and even living for yourself, you must live to please the one who created you. That is the secret of joy people of God as one man of God says "it's living for the audience of one." It's when you get to the place where only what your heavenly Father thinks matters to you. It's when you begin to live to please him that's the true secret of joy and gladness. It's when you can say as Jesus did in the Garden of Gethsemane not my will but your will be done. It's when you have no hidden agendas at all but to please the Father. When we love righteousness and hate iniquity we will walk in this joy. When we hate injustice and love justice we tap into this joy. I can hear the songwriter declaring, "this joy I have the world can't give it and the world can't take it away."

Many of God's people in this hour have allowed life to take its toll on them. As a result many are weak, some are depressed, some are emotionally and physically sick. I'm here today to tell you loud and clear according to Nehemiah 8:10, "The joy of the Lord is your strength." Your strength level is directly connected to your joy level. When we speak about joy we are talking about an internal thing that fills you with strength in spite of circumstances. Happiness is connected to circumstances we are talking joy. We are talking about something on the inside that is constant and it has power to even change outward circumstances. Sometimes things can look pretty hopeless but when you have this joy working inside you something in you will arise and say, "I will look unto Jesus who is the author and finisher of my faith who for the joy set before him endured the cross." Sometimes there are places in life we must visit that we don't enjoy but we must endure it in order to get to the place of joy set before us.

Joy will cause you to see life from an eternal perspective. Just to give you an example, if you are somewhat out of shape like I was being a former athlete you declare for the joy of chiseled muscles and a six pack I endure the track and the weights. Joy will cause you to have the end result in mind while you endure the temporary pain. Without joy and gladness working in your life, things that were only meant to be temporary will look like they will be in your life forever. When you lose your joy you lose your strength for living. You lose it because you lose focus, instead of being focused on Jesus your focus has become your circumstances. Whatever you meditate on in life it becomes your present reality. Why focus on that which is temporary and can be changed. Why not focus on what is eternal and has power to change temporary circumstances. One of the great lessons in life is to learn the only constant in life is God; everything else changes. In Nehemiah 8:9-12 "And Nehemiah, which is the Tirshatha (governor) and Ezra the priest, the scribe, and the Levites that taught the people, said unto all the people, This day is holy unto the Lord your God; mourn not, nor weep. For all the people wept, when they hear the words of the law. Then he said unto them, go your way, eat the fat, and drink the sweet, and send portions unto them for whom nothing is prepared: for this day is holy unto our Lord; neither be ye sorry; for the joy of the Lord is your strength. So the Levites stilled all the people saying, hold your peace, for the day is holy; neither be ye grieved. And all the people went their way to eat, and to drink, and to send portions, and to make great mirth, because they had understood the words that were declared unto them." These are some very powerful verses of scripture as well as the book of Nehemiah. We will have to do an in depth study at another time.

To sum things up Nehemiah led a project where the people of God rebuilt the walls around Jerusalem and during the building project in Chapter 8 the people asked Ezra the priest to bring the book of the law in order for it to be read. As Ezra stood to read the words of the law to the Israelites they stood attentive for several hours listening and they began to weep as they listened. As they wept and listened Nehemiah, Ezra the priest and the Levites declared to the people this day is holy to the Lord. They told the people not to be sorry or weep because the joy of the Lord is your strength. When a person gets born again, and the word of God becomes important in their lives, its time to rejoice. The people gave the wrong emotional response for what they heard. I don't know if like me you know many believers that never seem to be full of joy, something always seems to be wrong. Or do you know believers that are always talking about what's wrong with the church. In their own eyes they are Jeremiah, who was referred to as the weeping prophet. There is a time to sow prayer with tears, but it's not supposed to end with more tears. Psalms 126:5 states, "They that sow in tears shall reap in joy. It's time to be full of joy and serve the Lord with gladness. Jesus has defeated Satan, sins dominion has been conquered over the believer, its time to be full of joy." We are living in very stressful, depressed times in the world, but as believers we are in the world but not of it. We are called to be full of joy now. The Levites stopped the people from weeping and it says they understood the teaching. They understood it was not time for sorrow, it was time for joy, and the bible says they began to celebrate. I personally believe the church needs to do more celebrating. Our services should not feel dry and dead; Jesus is alive. We serve a risen Christ; the same spirit that raised Jesus from the dead lives in us our gatherings should be exciting and explosive. I declare to you it is time to get your joy back. It is time to serve the Lord with the oil of joy and gladness.

CHAPTER 10

THE JOY OF RIGHTEOUSNESS

AS WE CLOSE in this last chapter let's remember that the scepter of the kingdom is a scepter of righteousness. Just as a police officer has a badge that distinguishes them from another individual carrying a gun. Our badge in the kingdom saints is the gift of righteousness. Satan has power but we have authority, our power is legal because we have a badge. That badge or legal authority is that we are the righteousness of God in Christ. We are ambassadors for Christ in the earth; we have authority because of righteousness. Please remember sin causes us to break fellowship with the kingdom we represent. Please never forget this scripture I'm going to share with you. In James 4:7 it says, "Submit yourselves therefore to God, resist the devil, and he will flee from you." Notice the key to being able to resist the devil and seeing him flee from you is being submitted to God. In the gospel of John 1:1 it says "In the beginning was the Word, and the Word was with god and the Word was God." So I say to you today in order to submit to God we must submit to His Word. How do we submit? I'm glad you asked, in Romans 12:2 it says, "Be not conformed to this world but be ye transformed, by the renewing of your mind." In other words you have to allow the word to change how you think, because how you think determines how you behave. A person submitted to God will yield to what the Word of God has to say concerning any area of their life and allow thoughts contrary to the word in their mind to be stripped from them. The renewal of the mind involves changing how you see life and yielding your mind to what the word says. The level that you submit to what the word of God says will determine your ability to resist the devil in that area. When you submit to God the devil must run in terror because he no longer is just dealing with you but he must deal with the God in you; he is no match for our great God.

I want to share a scripture in Job that reveals to us the joy of righteousness. I want you to know a truth about having your righteousness restored. When you get your right standing with God back you have a right to recover what you may have lost when you operated in unrighteousness. In the book of Job it begins talking about how Job was an upright man, another term for righteous. He feared God and he stayed away from sin and evil. I really don't understand this modern day version of loving God and loving sin also. People of God when you truly love god you will not love sin. According to 1John 3:8 Satan is the original sinner, sin is part of his nature. To love God is also to hate evil. God allowed Satan to test Job or tempt him. The whole purpose was to bring Job to a new place in God. Job got to this new place of intimacy but it came by way of severe testing and trial. Job acquired great wealth in his life because God blessed the work of his hands. Satan came to prove to God if he were to take everything from Job he would not love and serve God. After Satan was allowed to attack Job's children with death, strip him of his possessions and damage his marriage. Job maintained his integrity; he stayed true to his worship of God. Job was fine, until his three friends came around to comfort him. In the process they try to convince Job that there is no way he could experience the trouble he was experiencing unless there was sin in his life. After his friends pressed Job severely and speak things about God that were not consistent with his nature, Job speaks up. He spends a lot of time proving to his friends that he was innocent and had not done anything wrong. Do you have any friends like Job's friends that think they know God but don't really know Him as well as they assume? Are you like Job, where you spend your time trying to prove yourself to people and declare your innocence? In other words like Job do you trust in your own righteousness, its called self-righteous.

Listen to this awesome promise in Isaiah 54:17 it says, "No weapon that is formed against thee shall prosper; and every tongue that shall rise against thee in judgment thou shalt condemn. This is the heritage of the servants of the Lord, and their righteousness is of me, saith the Lord." Every tongue that rises against thee shall be shown to be in the wrong is what thou shalt condemn means. Notice God says when it comes to the servants of the Lord he says their righteousness is of me. In self-righteousness there is no power, the power is in God's righteousness. Listen to Paul in Philippians 3:9, "And be found in Him, not having my own righteousness, which is of the law, but that which is through the faith of Christ, the righteousness which is of God by faith." Job and his three friends continue to share different opinions for quite awhile but then a young man named Elihu shows up that begins to speak inspired by the Spirit of God. In Job 3:3 Elihu begins to speak with great understanding given by God concerning what needs to take place for Job's life and his health to be restored.

In Job 33:19-28 in the Amplified Bible it says "God's voice may be heard by man when he is chastened with pain upon his bed and with continual strife in his bones or while all his bones are firmly set. So that his desire makes him loathe food, and even dainty dishes (nauseate him). His flesh is so wasted away that it cannot be seen, and his bones that were not seen stick out. Yes his soul draws near to corruption, and his life to the inflictors of death (the destroyers). (God's voice may be heard) if there is for the hearer a messenger or an angel, an interpreter, one among a thousand, to show to man what is right for him. (How to be upright and in right standing with God), Then God is gracious to him and says, deliver him from going down into the pit (of destruction). I have found a ransom (a price of redemption, an

atonement)! Then the mans flesh shall be restored; it becomes fresher and more tender than a child's; he returns to the days of his youth. He prays to God, and he is favorable to him, so that he sees his face with joy; for God restores to him his righteousness (his uprightness and right standing with God – with its joys). He looks upon other men or sings out to them I have sinned and perverted that, which was right, and it did not profit me, or he did not requite me (according to my iniquity)! God has redeemed my life from going down to the pit (of destruction), and my life shall see the light!

People of God this is such an amazing understanding of the power of righteousness. Notice starting from verse 19 no matter what state a person finds themselves in; they can even be close to death, through the power of righteousness they can be restored. If there be a messenger, an interpreter, one among a thousand, to show man how to be in right standing with God. In the Garden of Eden the trouble didn't start for man until he lost righteousness. Once man lost his righteousness then sin began to directly affect mans life. I got good news for you; Jesus came to give us our right standing with the Father back. When we get born again we receive the gift of righteousness, which is nothing less than the righteousness of Christ Himself. In verse 24 after man gets his righteousness back it says then God is gracious unto im. In other words He extends grace in the life of the person who gets their righteousness back. Then God says deliver him from going down into the pit of destruction. I want to declare to you whatever pits of destruction you are in get ready to be delivered. In Psalms 34:19 it says "Many are the afflictions of the righteous but the Lord delivereth them out of them all." Many are the trials, tests, troubles of the righteous but you shall come out of them all.

In Job we must remember after Satan attacked him he was smote with boils from the top of his head to the souls of his feet. He was so sick he was not functioning at normal capacity. Elihu, by the spirit of God, begins to declare Job's deliverance was very possible and he could without doubt be restored. In verse 24 of Job 33 we find our answer in the Amplified Bible. God is gracious and says deliver him; I have a ransom (a price of redemption, an atonement). A ransom is a price paid to secure the freedom of a slave or to set free from liability and charges, and the ransom pays a price for redemption. Redemption is being released from a penalty by the payment of a price, and then given a right standing with God. The word atonement is at-one-ment, the state of being at one or being reconciled. It also means to make satisfaction for his offenses. The god news of the gospel is Jesus was the ransom we need. He paid the price for us to be redeemed, he paid for us with his life, and he offered his body and his blood. Jesus has redeemed us; He made atonement for us He was offered as a sacrifice for sin. When He becomes our Lord and savior He imparts to us the gift of righteousness. God clearly declares in these verses the answer for man's deliverance and restoration is making right standing available again. Now that the price is paid for sin and righteousness is restored, verse 25 says the man's flesh shall be restored. Right standing with God positions a person for restoration.

The great news about restoration is when you are restored things are much better than they were before. It's time for you to lay claim to full restoration you are the righteousness of God in Christ. Notice God doesn't just heal the man's body to where he was before, he makes it fresher and more tender than a child's, he returns to the days of his youth. Get ready because you have your righteousness back, it's time for Full Restoration, Full Recovery, all because the price for sin has been paid. You have a legal right according to the Word of God for full restoration, claim your restoration now child of God, you have rights in Christ. In Psalm 107:2 it says, "Let the redeemed of the Lord say so, whom he hath redeemed from the hand of the enemy." The key to accessing the benefits of redemption is your faith you must say so. How does righteousness, which is of faith work according to the Word of God? Does it work by keeping rituals and religious works? Of course not! In Romans 10:8-10 it says, "But what saith it? The word is nigh thee, even in thy mouth, and in thy heart: that is, the word of faith, which we preach; That if thou shalt confess with thy mouth the Lord Jesus, and shalt believe in thou heart that God hath raised him from the dead, thou shalt be saved. For with the heart man believeth unto righteousness: and with the mouth confession is made unto salvation." Notice we believe with the heart but we confess (or say so) with the mouth. You must use faith to receive what is already made available. You believe and then you confirm your belief by what you say. In verse 26 of Job it says he prays to God and he is favorable to him. Notice when the man has his right standing with God restored his access to God is also restored. He prays unto God and He listens and responds to his prayer. For God restores to him his righteousness, his uprightness and right standing with God with its joys.

There are joys that come with right living. The oil of joy comes with right living. Right living is much more rewarding than wrong living, never believe the picture the world paints. Right living will produce life and peace. Wrong living produces sin and death. Righteousness is what's needed in order to come out of defeat in to victory. Please remember that righteousness doesn't exempt you from trials and trouble. Oftentimes trouble comes because you are living right. But remember your God said He would deliver you out of them all. In Psalms 37:39-40 it says,

"But the salvation of the righteous is of the Lord: He is their strength in the time of trouble, and the Lord shall help them, and deliver them: he shall deliver them from the wicked, and save them, because they trust in him." The Word of God is filled with promise after promise as it relates to the righteous, oh the joys of righteousness! When you walk in righteousness you will never be defeated. In Psalms 103:2 we are encouraged not to forget his benefits. There are many benefits that come to the man and woman who walks in the righteousness that God gives as a gift through Christ. In verse 27 in Job it says the man who has experienced the joy of righteousness will testify of God's goodness. He will declare, "I have sinned and perverted that which was right, and it did not profit me." But the awesome news is the price of sin has been paid, righteousness has been made available, now it's time for deliverance. This same man will declare according to verse 28, "God has redeemed my life from going down to the pit of destruction that he may be enlighten with the light of the living." You can now declare, "I shall not die but, live to declare the works of the Lord." You must realize when you experience this level of grace and mercy you must let it be known all over. What God has done for you He wants to do the same for so many others. He does it for others as you let them know what He has done for you. He will restore to you His righteousness with its joys!

CHAPTER 11

THE WELLS OF SALVATION

"AND THERE SHALL come forth a rod out of the stem of Jesse, and a Branch shall grow out of his roots: and the spirit of the Lord shall rest upon him, the spirit of wisdom and understanding, the spirit of counsel and might, the spirit of knowledge and of the fear of the Lord; And shall make him of quick understanding in the fear of the Lord: and he shall not judge after the sight of his eyes, neither reprove after the hearing of his ears: But with righteousness shall he judge the poor, and reprove with equity for the week of the earth: and he shall smite the earth with the rod of his mouth, and with the breath of his lips shall he slay the wicked. And righteousness shall be the girdle of his loins, and faithfulness the girdle of his reins." (Isaiah)

Notice righteousness is being compared to as a belt around the waist area that holds all things in place or together. Notice this branch out of Jesse who was David's father would have righteousness as the girdle of his loins. This is none other than Jesus Christ, which possesses the scepter of his kingdom. As we take a look at the 12th Chapter of Isaiah I want you to really pay close attention to the awesome power in this small chapter. In Isaiah 12 it says "And in that day thou shalt say, O Lord, I will praise thee: though thou wast angry with me, thine anger is turned away, and thou comfort me. Behold, God is my salvation; I will trust, and not be afraid: For the Lord JEHOVAH is my strength and my song; He also is become my salvation. Therefore with joy shall ye draw water out of the wells of salvation. And in that day shall ye say, Praise the Lord, call upon His name, declare His doings among the people, make mention that His name is exalted. Sing unto the Lord; for He hath done excellent things: this is known in all the earth. Cry out and shout, thou inhabitant of Zion: for great is the Holy One of Israel in the midst of thee."

People of God our view of God must change under the new covenant. In Romans 5:1 it says, "Therefore being justified by faith, we have peace with God through our Lord Jesus Christ." In Isaiah 12:1 we are told God was angry but his anger was turned away and as a result it says I will praise you. Not only do we praise you because your wrath has been satisfied but now His mercy is extended, it says we are comforted. There is no comfort in the world to be compared to the comfort of our God. The Holy Spirit is even referred to as the Comforter. Jesus promised His disciples He would not leave them comfortless, thank god for the Comforter. Then in verse 2 it declares that god is my salvation, I will trust and not be afraid. Jehovah is my strength, He is become my salvation. The name Jehovah is the name of God connected to redemption. We have what's called His Jehovahistic name. Here are the names and what they mean:

1. Jehovah – Jireh   (Lord will provide)

2. Jehovah – Rapha   (Lord who heals you)

3. Jehovah – Nissi   (Lord our banner)

4. Jehovah – Qadash   (Lord who sanctifies)

5. Jehovah – Shalom   (Lord our peace)

6. Jehovah – Tsidkenu (Lord our righteousness)

In Jeremiah 23:6 it says He will be called the Lord

Our righteousness.

7. Jehovah – Shammah (Lord is present)

8. Jehovah – Raah (Lord is my shepherd)

All of these names find their fulfillment in the name of Jesus. Notice according to Jeremiah the Lord if our righteousness. We are to sing and rejoice because Jehovah has become our salvation. In verse 3 it says with joy shall we draw forth waters out of the wells of salvation. Without joy you can't draw forth the waters.

I'm telling you people of God we need our joy back. It's time for us to be excited about the salvation Jehovah has made available to us. We can never truly enjoy it without the fruit of joy. When you have your joy back it will change how you view life. I'm declaring today that your joy be made full. A life full of joy. Even in the midst of trials I'm declaring that you rejoice right in the middle of it. There must be joy to the world because the Lord has come. He who is the author of joy lives inside of every believer. I'm telling you when you learn to rejoice you tap into the internal well that God has put in you. Because the well is in you springing up into everlasting life be full of joy now. Speak to yourself in psalms, and hymns, and in spiritual songs, making melody in your hearts to the Lord. According to verse 4 it's time to praise the Lord and declare His deeds among the people. We must be believers full of joy sharing His love amongst the world. Don't let the devil, trials, circumstances or life have your joy. Get your joy back now. Even if sin or a struggle you have encountered has robbed you of your joy just simply go to your father and get forgiveness. Remember the price for sin is already paid for Jesus paid the price for sin whether it's past, present or future its been paid for. You have no excuse not to get your joy back. Right standing with God comes with joy. I'm declaring to you now according to Psalm 51verse 12 God is restoring to you the joy of salvation. Once your joy has been restored let me share with you a secret to keep your joy full. As you live a spirit filled life you stay full of joy. If you really want to experience the joy of salvation constantly there is what's called soul winners joy. Do you know the feeling of leading someone else to righteousness by faith? When you experience seeing someone go from unrighteous to receiving righteousness by faith when they are born again, it's an incredible rush of joy. I declare today you will experience the joy of salvation like you have never before. It's your time to move in kingdom authority the scepter of the kingdom is in your hand!

CHAPTER 12

THE SCEPTER IS IN YOUR HAND

GENESIS 49: 8-10 says, "Judah thou art he whom thy brother shall praise: thy hand shall be in the neck of thine enemies; thy father's children shall bow down before thee. Judah is a lion's whelp (cub): from the prey, my son, thou art gone up: he stooped down; he couched as a lion, and as an old lion; who shall rouse him up? The scepter shall not depart from Judah, nor a lawgiver from between his feet, until Shiloh come; and unto him shall the gathering of the people be. What prophetic verses of scripture listen to verse 10 in the Amplified Bible. In verse 10 it says, "The scepter or leadership shall not depart from Judah, nor the ruler's staff from between his feet, until Shiloh (TheMessiah, the Peaceful One) comes to whom it belongs, and to him shall be the obedience of the people." Jacob one of the patriarchs, the grandson of Abraham and son of Isaac is about to die but before he does he gathers his sons around his bed. He began to declare to his sons that represent the next generation what their prophetic destiny would be. He speaks a word over each of them so they would know their future. Fathers especially in the Old Testament would declare the blessing over the lives of the next generation. As he speaks over the life of his son Judah he declares some power prophetic words over his life. At Judah's birth his mother declared for this son I will praise the Lord, so his name means praise. In

I Peter 2:9 it says, "but you are a chosen generation, a royal priesthood, an holy nation, a peculiar people; that ye should show forth the praises of him who hath called you out of darkness into his marvelous light. As believers in Christ we are called to praise the Lord with the lives we live and also with the breath we have. In Psalms 150 it declares let everything that has breath praise the Lord. Jacob declares to Judah his brethren shall praise him because his hand shall be on the neck of his enemies. After the death of Joshua in Judges Chapter 1 there was no single leader prepared to lead Israel as Joshua did when Moses died. So they asked God a question in verse 1:20 of Judges, it says "Now after the death of Joshua it came to pass, that the children of Israel asked the Lord, saying, who shall go up for us against the Canaanites first, to fight against them? And the Lord said, Judah shall go up: behold, I have delivered the land into his hand." The prophetic declaration is send praise first I have delivered the land in the hand of the praisers. Saints of God when you learn to bless the Lord at all times you will see victory after victory. Saints of God this tribe of Judah in the bible is spoken about more than any other tribe. David the King is linked to the tribe of Judah, when he became king he first reigned over Judah for seven years then all of Israel for 33 years II Samuel 5:4-5.

The bible is emphatic that we are in a spiritual battle and not a physical one. We don't wrestle against flesh and blood but against principalities, powers, the rulers of the darkness of this world and spiritual wickedness in heavenly places, Ephesians 6:12. And then II Corinthians 10:3-5 lets us know that we must use spiritual weapons to win in this war. Our victory has come through the cross of Christ but we must appropriate that victory as believers. One of the greatest weapons we have been given is praise. When you make your mind up that you will walk by faith and not by sight you discover that praise is the voice of faith. You praise God because the work is already done; you praise him because he is great and almighty. You praise him because your hand will grab a hold of the neck of any demon. You praise him because you already have the victory. You throw off the garment of depression, defeat and a failing spirit. And instead you put on the garment of praise expressive of victory and gratitude. You praise him because Jesus has already conquered satan, sin and death. You praise him because Judah has been prophetically declared victorious!

I want you to know prophetically many of God's people have walked in defeat instead of victory because of sin and disobedience. In Lamentations 1:3 it says, "Judah is gone into captivity because of affliction, and because of great servitude: she dwelleth among the heathen, she finds no rest: all her persecutors overlook her between the straits. In the amplified bible it says Judah has gone into exile (to escape) from the affliction and laborious servitude (of the homeland). Saints of God there is affliction you experience for Christ's sake, and there is affliction you experience because of satanic attack. I'm declaring to you today you are being made free from satanic attack. Instead of trouble, distress, depression, frustration, today you get your praise back. The joy of the Lord is your strength you have been chosen for victory. I don't care what satanic affliction has come against you the Lord is about to deliver you out of them all. Then in Nahum 1:9 it says, "What do ye imagine against the Lord? He will make an utter end: affliction shall not rise up the second time. Do you hear this child of God; affliction shall not rise up the second time. I want you to declare today what you have gone through will not rise up the second time. I want you to know what you have gone through you will never go through it again. Come on use your faith and declare, **"I will not go through the second time."**

As you come out of it say bye to it because you will never see it again. Come on faith comes by the Word receive this word right now if you are a parent and you went through with the first child declare its not coming to the second. If you have been divorced declare you will not go through this in your new marriage. Use your faith people of God and declare affliction shall not rise up the second time. If you are in the ministry I want to declare to you what you have gone through you will not go through it in your ministry for the second time. Men of God, woman of God get ready for breakthrough!

As we prepare to close I want to take you back to Genesis 49:10, It says the scepter or leadership shall not depart from Judah. The scepter of the kingdom has been placed in the hands of praises. It's in the hands of those that have allowed themselves to be separated by God for priestly ministry; A ministry of showing forth the praise of him who has called us out of darkness into his marvelous light. Those that will lead the church into the 21st century are those with the scepter in their hand. It's people who walk in the gift of righteousness; those who live a life that is separated and consecrated to their God. A people who lift up holy hands and lead by example as true praisers of God are suppose to do. I want you to know in this hour we will be led by the lion of the tribe of Judah whose army's all dressed in white fine linen will follow. The fine linen is the righteousness of the saints; those with the scepter in their hand. As their king moves, they move, as their king issues a decree they decree.

In this hour there is a people called the remnant that will possess the scepter, get ready to see the king display His glory in the earth such as we have never seen on this magnitude. Our King declares from Haggai 2:6-9 "**For thus saith the Lord of Hosts, Yet once it is a little while, and I will shake the heavens, and the earth, and the sea, and the dry land; And I will shake all nations, and the desire of all nations shall come: and I will fill this house with glory, saith the Lord** of Hosts. The silver is mine, and the gold is mine, saith the Lord of Hosts. The glory of this latter house shall be greater than of the former, saith the Lord of Hosts: and in this place will I give peace, saith the Lord of Hosts.